PRAISE FOR
INHERITING MAGIC

"Jennifer Love Hewitt takes us on a journey of love, loss, and self-realization in her book *Inheriting Magic*. One part self-help, one part memoir, and one part how-to, Jennifer manages to straddle three different genres, giving all moms a treasure trove of ideas with a healthy dose of heart. You will laugh, you will cry, you will never make breakfast the same way again. Disclaimer: I drank an entire liter of moon water before writing this endorsement."

—**Jenny Mollen, actor, *New York Times* bestselling author of *City of Likes* and *I Like You Just the Way I Am***

"*Inheriting Magic* will inspire you to become the most magical version of yourself. It guides and teaches you how to bring magic into your home and family in ways you've never thought of before. It made me remember to be magical and to live life to the fullest. No holding back!"

—**Amanda Kloots, cohost of *The Talk* and *New York Times* bestselling author of *Live Your Life***

INHERITING MAGIC

JENNIFER LOVE HEWITT

INHERITING MAGIC

My Journey Through Grief, Joy, Celebration, and Making Every Day Magical

BenBella Books, Inc.

DALLAS, TX

BenBella Books, Inc.
8080 N. Central Expressway
Suite 1700
Dallas, TX 75206
benbellabooks.com
Send feedback to feedback@benbellabooks.com

BenBella is a federally registered trademark.

Printed in China
10 9 8 7 6 5 4 3 2

Library of Congress Control Number: 2024013485
ISBN 9781637745953 (hardcover)
ISBN 9781637745960 (ebook)

Editing by Rick Chillot
Copyediting by Michael Fedison
Proofreading by Sarah Vostok and Isabelle Rubio
Text design and composition by Endpaper Studio
Cover design by Sarah Avinger
Illustrations on front cover, page xvi, and page 90 by Vanessa Rivera
Reference photography for front cover, page xvi, and page 90 by Sam McGuire
Photography on pages 113 and 120 by Sam McGuire
Holiday Junkie calendar on page 93 by Emily King

Special discounts for bulk sales are available. Please contact bulkorders@benbellabooks.com.

This book is dedicated to my babies, Autumn, Atticus, and Aidan,
who show me that life is magical every day;

to my mom who taught me magic is possible;

and to my husband, Brian,
who I knew was magic the day we met.

"But all the magic I have known, I've had to make myself."

—*SHEL SILVERSTEIN*

CONTENTS

PREFACE

In June 2012 I was asked to attend a TV festival in Monaco. My mom had been diagnosed with cancer in February; she'd had surgery, started chemotherapy, and was feeling hopeful. My mom and I had been to Monaco together before, and had an amazing time. She loved to travel and begged me to go on this trip because she couldn't, but this time I didn't want to go. So we decided that we would plan her cancer-free party before I left for the airport. It would be our biggest party yet! It helped us both to see the light at the end of the cancer tunnel. Something just didn't feel right that day about leaving, but it would only be a few quick days, and then back to party planning. That was our promise to each other. Before I took off, I texted my mom a picture of me holding champagne and said, "Cheers!" She texted back, "Cheers!" with a picture of her in a silly rainbow wig filter. It was perfect. It was her.

But it was the last exchange I would have with my mom.

After landing in Monaco, I turned on my phone and saw three missed calls from a phone number I didn't recognize. There was a message from my mom's friend: "She had a rough night and got very sick. She's in the hospital." I knew deep down that I shouldn't have left her, and that I would never forgive myself.

As I tried to get more information, the hours passed. My brother was on his way to Los Angeles, but I couldn't get a flight out until the next morning. My mother was in a coma and doctors were giving her a 20 percent chance to make it. It felt like a nightmare, and I was begging to wake up. My mom and I were planning our biggest party yet. This couldn't be happening. I was able to get the next flight out and made it home, but never got the chance to say goodbye.

I'd walked out of her front door hopeful and laughing, and now I could barely walk in because she was gone. My whole life changed. I changed.

Later, in processing my grief, I began to feel very deeply that my mom and I weren't supposed to say goodbye. We were supposed to be laughing, planning a party, and excited for the joy it would bring us and others. That's what we loved to do, and in our last moment together that's what we did. We planned one hell of a party. I found myself through grief—as a wife, mommy, magic-maker, and *Holiday Junkie*.

♥ This image by the amazing Vanessa Rivera is very special to me. Autumn is the little version of me releasing my mom to heaven, symbolized by the hummingbird, as the adult me looks on from inside the plane never wanting to let her go. The stickers on the suitcase are my mom's favorite places to travel.

1.

INHERITING MAGIC

As I sat down to write this book, I needed to remember *how* I became so addicted to joy, and *when* I started having an obsessive dependency on magic. The truth is, when I was growing up, magic was created for me. I thought everyone lived that way, and as I got older it became clear they didn't. The everyday world wasn't magical, but my mom made sure our little world was.

It wasn't until I began to write this that I realized: my mom used magic to deal with grief. It was also how she expressed her love, through special moments, thoughtful touches, and a deep belief that even in hard times magic could exist. My parents got divorced when I was six months old, and my brother was nine years old. My mom moved past her pain and turned it into creating joy, magic, and explosive love for us every day.

When my mom passed, I was convinced all the magic she created, and that I experienced with her, was gone. Magic would be something in my past. And for the first time, magic couldn't help me through the incredible pain I was feeling. I remember my first Christmas without her. I took a train ride alone to New York City, which I had never done before, and I didn't want to listen to Christmas music that I loved. I stayed in a friend's beautiful apartment, in a part of the city my mom and I hadn't visited before. It had not one Christmas decoration . . . and that was for the best. Because not even the New York City lights could create the Christmas my mom did. I met up with my brother and his family on Christmas Eve, and ate Chinese food in an empty restaurant instead of tamales in my mom's kitchen. And I remember waking up on Christmas morning thinking, we did it! We made it through the first big holiday without her. I had no idea that the following holiday season, I would be a mom for the first time.

A year later we celebrated our first Christmas in our new home. We just got married the month before and had our first

baby. It was the most special time. The grief was still very present, but the joy of starting our family filled my heart in a way that made magic feel possible again. Brian hung beautiful lights in our bedroom that gave the sleepless nights with a newborn a soft Christmas glow. My mom's ornaments looked perfect on our tree, but it was hard knowing she wouldn't be there to see them. And in the making of new memories that Christmas, something I lost came back to me. In December 2013, I became the Holiday Junkie.

Without me knowing it at the time, my mom was teaching me how to create my own magic. I could create it anytime, and that's when I would feel her the most. I believe it's our duty as magic-makers to pass it on when we go, leaving it behind for others to experience so it always lives on. In grieving I thought I lost that magic because I lost her. Instead, she left me with an unforgettable gift that she imprinted into my heart—her magic.

My Mom's Magic

My mom's magic is truly hard to put into words. It was a feeling she created not only on holidays, but on any random Thursday if the mood hit her that day. I remember as a teenager being present in all the special moments that she created for us and for those around us, but I also remember, as I got older, enjoying the moments when I could take in all that she was and how it made people feel. When we were kids, it was in small things, like leaving school early on a random day to eat, play, and bond. As a teen, it was when I would come to her with a broken heart, and she would put up Christmas lights in my room to make me smile. There were silly times, like the Christmas when she had been traveling a lot and thought it would be funny to only give us gifts from the airport shops, or things she could buy on a flight! We were a little confused about that one, but she presented them so

The photo of my mom is from when she modeled as a teenager, and her smile is infectious. The photo of us underneath is at our favorite restaurant in New York City, Campagnola. We went on every trip we took to the city. The one of me on her back is in a field of bluebonnets in Texas. It's one of my favorite pics of us together. She was so beautiful.

well! "This is a magical scarf because it was purchased 35,000 feet in the air!" I wasn't sold, but her love of life and adventure made that scarf my favorite.

Thanksgiving was magical, because I never knew exactly who would be joining us. Family, of course, but my mom also would invite anyone who couldn't get home to family or who didn't want to get home to family. The second they walked in the door, it was Thanksgiving (or Friendsgiving) joy, and everyone felt like they belonged nowhere else but there. The food, drinks, and gorgeous table were all set to make memories, bring laughter, and so much joy. Anyone who joined us was so deeply grateful. She would glow with knowing she had made it all come together.

One year on Christmas she made it snow in her front yard, and it was so magical, but the part she loved the most was when all the kids in the neighborhood stopped by. She sat by the window most of that day watching them play, and convinced them that of all the homes in Los Angeles it had only snowed in her yard. She'd found a snow company recommended by someone on the set of *Ghost Whisperer*, and they showed up at 7 am and made it snow! Her whole front yard and the sidewalk outside were covered. It was magical and special. It was so her. Years later, after I had my own kids, I decided one year to reach out to that same company and I made it snow on *our* front lawn for Christmas. I surprised my kids with snow gear and told them to look outside. They looked at me the same way I must've looked at my mom: in awe of how I made that happen and so grateful for the magic. It was the most fun day, and one of the many times I would use her magic to re-create joy like I'd had, for my kids.

My mom also made simple and daily traditions for us. I had very early calls for work most of the time, and because I lived across the street from her, she would have me come over and we would hold hands before I went to work at 4 am. She wanted me to feel connected to her love and support for my very long workdays. I would give anything to hold her hand right now. After she passed, I was contacted by so many people. They were strangers to me, but not to her. They met her on her travels, and she made them feel special. They all said the same thing: she was the brightest light and made them feel like they were friends. That's how I knew they had actually met her. My mom's magic was made of thoughtful ideas, extra attention paid to details, and a deep need and belief that she could make you feel better than ever before, and she did.

Deep Breaths and a Little Magic

After my mom passed, it felt like I had held my breath for weeks. It was as if I had to learn to breathe again in the months following her death. Deep long breaths. We had so much to do and take care of. It was overwhelming. Thank God my brother and sister-in-law stayed to help with everything. We all had tasks and things that needed to be done to pack up her things, her home, and all of our memories. Brian and I were new in our relationship, and it meant so much that he came to help and spend time with my family. He was a phenomenal support system for me.

It's strange, but you really get to know someone in a new way when packing all of their personal belongings. I lived across the street from my mom, and I knew in my gut that if I stayed there, looking at her empty house every day and trying to continue to live what was our life together alone, I would truly drown in my grief. My brother and his family would have to return home at some point, friends would stop bringing food and checking in as much because life must go on, and I felt so deeply in my gut that I had to move on too.

So I sold our houses and found a place in a part of LA that I'd never lived in, and started fresh. She came with me in my heart, but all the memories we made, and the shared experiences—like places we ate together, and how we decorated the walls of my home—would be replaced with new versions of what life would be now. Here is where the magic began, and I think I have my mom to thank. I found a place available in a building my mom and I had looked at once before her passing. When I went to see it, they said it was called the Condo in the Sky, and it was as close to heaven as you can get. For them that meant the top floor, and it was really nice, but for me it meant closer to where my best friend now lived, and where I would start again on my own. Magic.

Brian was truly incredible during what was the toughest time in my life. He was with me for bad days, good days, and days of truly not knowing what I felt. Another bit of magic transpired with my mom and Brian before she passed, when he came to my birthday party and my mom asked him to dance. It was so cute, and something about it felt so special. It was the only time he would meet her, or see her, before she passed, but my mom and I discussed him often. She knew that how I felt about him was different, and she told me to love with my heart open and

We got engaged in Italy in our friend's apartment. We sent this photo out and one of our friends sent it back to us with these cute words attached. It was so exciting. I was going to marry the man of my dreams!

not to worry. If it was meant to be, it would be. The day I flew to Monaco, which would be the last day I would see my mom, she gave me a little ring with the initial *B* on it. I was wearing it when she died, and it gave me an immense amount of comfort that we had such a nice conversation about him that day. She saw what I felt for him. It was love. Again, magic.

I moved, was in love, grieved, and was back at work. It was truly surreal. I happened to be directing an episode of *The Client List* when one day I felt like I was coming down with the flu. Which wasn't completely out of the ordinary, because I was working a lot and going through a lot emotionally from losing her. But I was also mysteriously glowing, yet very tired. It struck me to take a pregnancy test, truly just because, and that was it. That moment our lives changed forever. It wasn't the flu . . . it was our little girl!

Oh man, I loved pregnancy. I'd never had that kind of time to connect with myself, and to just be, to eat and sleep, and even though it hurt so badly doing it without my mom, I was going to get that relationship that is so precious and so special with my own little girl. It was magical. Labor was intense! Talk about learning to take deep breaths . . . but it was also incredible. Brian,

Brian and I truly couldn't wait to be parents. I used to send him pics of me on the couch growing our little human. We, of course, had to take pregnancy photos and my friend took this one that I love!

When Autumn was born, she was only 5 pounds, 4 ounces, and they called her "take-home size," which made us laugh. She loved to be close to my heartbeat and tucked in my nightgown when she first came home. This picture melts me.

again, was amazing. The way he held space for me during labor, but also showed up for me and our little girl, meant everything. I will never forget how proud he was of me.

Postpartum was difficult. In the following days, it was milk stains and hormones mixed with grief and longing for my mother to meet our little girl. Every great moment in my life was a re-minder that she was gone. But as days and months went by, I could feel her. I saw her in my daughter and the connection we were making.

Time for more magic! I went back to work when Autumn was eight months old, and I took her with me. I would sit with her in the back seat while my friend drove us to work—that was the only time I had to learn my lines. I would breastfeed her in be-tween takes, and pretend I was thriving, but the truth is I wanted to be home catching up on sleep, playing with my daughter, and learning to be a mom. I was hoping work would feel the same, but it didn't. I was a different person now. My life was different.

On a day off, my friend Nikki and I danced in unicorn one-sies—as you do on days off—and she looked at me and said, "Wouldn't it be crazy if you were in a unicorn onesie and pregnant again?" I still don't know why she said it, but something in me told me to take a test. And sure enough, it was time for Atticus. This meant I would now be driving to work while feeding our eight-month-old, and growing a whole new human!

It was a great pregnancy, but the grief that I thought had healed a little came right back. My mom would never walk through our door and meet our babies. I took a little break from work after Atticus was born to just be a mom. Mommy and Me classes, mac and cheese–stained T-shirts, potty training, and so much joy. All I had ever wanted was to be a mom, and it was even better than I could've even imagined. Autumn and Atticus became best friends from day one and it has been the most beautiful and wild ride. Brian and I watched as two incredible souls turned into the coolest humans. We created a family we are proud of. We made incredible memories even in the midst of the pandemic.

And then it was time for one more big change: deep breaths and, you guessed it, magic.

I was watching TV with the kids one night and a commercial for the Clearblue pregnancy test came on. Atticus out of nowhere said, "Mommy, you should pee on one of those in case you have a baby in your belly." It was so weird and random, I couldn't stop thinking about it. So, I ordered a test on Amazon and hid it from everyone including Brian and . . . when I took it, the word took my breath away: *pregnant*! In a pandemic, while playing a pregnant person on TV! How did Atticus know?

I had zero symptoms, but it was our baby on the way, and Autumn and Atticus had wanted this so badly. I was going to give them the best present ever! It was the most beautiful pregnancy. My big kids took such good care of me. It was really special for them to see him grow in my belly, watch me change, and see all

The first morning coffee after having Atticus and being a mommy of two. I was in pure bliss. Autumn loved to reach up and touch my belly and say hi to the baby. The bottom pic was our first Christmas as a family of four! Exhausted, but happy and blessed.

Aidan was our magical surprise. The pic of me with the pee stick I took before anyone in the house knew I was pregnant, although Atticus had a hunch. The pic of the kids was taken right after they found out. I had to document another awesome pregnancy belly and how quickly my clothes didn't fit with baby number three. The pic with the beach behind me was taken on our baby moon for Aidan. We took the big kids on an amazing road trip to Carmel. One of our best trips ever!

that goes into a mommy getting a baby here safe and sound. I felt my mom the most during my labor with Aidan, and this time the grief presented as really just longing for her to be here and see them all.

Postpartum hit again. I still haven't bounced back in my body, and I am very much still learning to be the mom of three kids, but I am so grateful and now we are a party of five! Aidan has been the most special blessing. We all love him so much and don't know how we went this long without him. He's our baby. I've taken a lot of deep breaths over the last eleven years and have reflected on the fact that I've been given a whole lot of magic. I see my mom's magic in all of my kids, and although she isn't here to share it with us, I am certain she is watching over us from above, proud of the family we've grown out of love and . . . magic.

Turning Grief into Magic

One of the things I struggled with the most when grieving was how to keep my mom present for my kids. I had all my memories of her, and knew her so deeply, that she would always be with me. But for my kids, that wasn't possible.

My mom was a lover of the world. Traveling was her happy place, and she found her best self in all the places she would travel to and the people she would meet. She loved to dance with strangers and make new friends. On every trip, she would spend a week at the pool learning the stories of the people around her. Anyone lucky enough to meet her on one of her adventures saw her truly happy, alive, and free, full of wonder and joy. She was like a hummingbird, always so busy and buzzing, beautiful, captivating, going from one adventure to the next. I knew that's who she had to be to my children. They had to understand they couldn't meet her in person, so we took our grief for her and turned it into magic. She was now our hummingbird.

They see her everywhere: school, parks, our backyard, road trips, and they know deep inside that Mimi is always with us. It's also how I see her now. My little hummingbird, still so busy with adventure, checking in on us, and alive in a new way. The hummingbird has been known to be a signal that hard times are over and healing can begin. I believe that to be true. My kids really feel my mom with them, and that for me is everything. Always my mom. Forever their Mimi. For life, our hummingbird.

You Can't Lock Magic Down

March 17, 2020. Our morning started with one last attempt at catching a leprechaun before moving to our new house. We didn't catch him, but we certainly had fun trying. As we made our way to our new home, we saw a rainbow. It felt like magic was in the air, and for us it was. New energy, new rooms to make memories in, and of course new places for me to decorate for holidays. At that time, we had no idea that as we moved into our new home the world would be moving into lockdown. Before moving into a new space, I set intentions for us: more time together, more memories, more small moments to know each other and discover ourselves as a family. All of that was definitely on the horizon, but in a way I never expected.

As the weeks, months, and a full year went by, we watched as the world changed around us. Fear, passion, anger, loss, and anxiety were some of the things we would have to talk about and understand as a family. But at the same time, we created new memories and held on to our deep belief in all things magical. We had dance parties, worked on tons of Legos and puzzles, made food, and even allowed the kids to use their scooters inside the house, to create a roller skating rink feel. We snuggled and watched movies, all sleeping in the same room, and the kids set up tents in a room that had no furniture that they named "Whoatown," a safe city with no Covid and lots of toys and snacks. (We still call that room Whoatown, for the record.) I decorated the house for every holiday, of course, and even on random Thursdays for dinner. We had driveway parties so we could see our neighbors, if from a distance. We had picnics in the back of Daddy's truck, and we figured out how to make candy stations in the yard so the kids still got to trick-or-treat for Halloween when it wasn't possible to do the real thing. Brian and I filled the house with lots of music, him on guitar and me on vocals, and the kids would come in and out of the room, sometimes joining in. We navigated Zoom school and held on to faith that one day the world would go back to normal.

When Brian and I got married in 2013, it was just the two of us in our backyard. It was truly one of our most special moments. And when we moved in 2020, we both felt sad that we wouldn't be able to look into the new backyard and picture the day we got married. So, as Covid grew more intense and magic-making and making memories became our mode of survival, I decided

to find the guy who married us, and asked him to do it again. I had my two mini Holiday Junkies to help set up, reached out to some friends for food delivery and cute furniture, and voila, we had a sweet little backyard wedding. Autumn and Atticus stood with us and held our hands as we said our vows. They loved the wedding cake the most! It was special for them to see us as a couple making promises to not only each other but to them as well. Now, when Brian and I look out into our new backyard, we can say we got married right in that spot. It wasn't a magical time in the world at all, but in our little backyard of the world, it was full of magic.

Eventually, I got the call that I had to go back to work, which felt so intense. People who I'd known and enjoyed so much throughout the years now had masked faces I couldn't see. Fear of so many unknowns led our reality. Then, as if the entire world changing weren't enough, our little world changed for the better. I found out Aidan would be joining our family. I was pregnant! The most extraordinary moment of my life was being able to show my kids what my body could do during pregnancy. How it would grow and change and that I was bringing them a sibling. They took such good care of me, and were in awe of how my belly changed and grew. Aidan arrived and my kids truly became the most incredible siblings, and such a huge help to Mommy and Daddy.

When I ask my kids about their thoughts on the quarantine, they share their feelings of anxiety and fear during that time. Of course, they didn't love Zoom school, and it was hard not seeing friends as much. But they also say it was the best time ever. They loved having us just *be* with them, creating memories, traditions, silly moments, and truly just *being* together. They say they will always remember it as a tough time, but also a special one, and so will we. As adults, we don't think we can stop everything and just live. We are always searching for something, or trying to create the next thing, trying to give our kids everything. We don't believe it's okay to just take a break, but it is. My kids just wanted *us*. Our time. It's deeply valuable for our children and our families if we can stop and just create a little magic every now and then (hopefully without the world falling apart).

We spent the first year in our new home creating the energy it now holds, making magic on any day we could, laughing, singing, dancing, creating traditions, and trying new things. We unpacked so much more than just our boxes. We made memories in every room. We filled the space with love and hope, and we made lockdown magic.

Little Bits of Magic

Aidan will be turning two soon. And ever since he was born, magic has been a part of his story. He was an August baby, and within three weeks of him being here I had him in a pumpkin patch for photos. We laughed because, for the first five months of his life, every time he napped he would wake up to new decorations or a full switch to the next holiday. He really started taking great naps in early December, and would fall asleep to Michael Bublé singing "It's Beginning to Look a Lot Like Christmas." And to this day, *still*, that's his song. It's so sweet when you hear it playing in the house and know Aidan is ready to nap. Aidan has also recently started walking around the house with a Harry Potter wand saying, "Magic mama! Magic!" My heart is truly filled with joy because I know he already feels it. In his heart he knows his house is a little different, and is filled with magic.

This year, Autumn and Atticus asked to make vision boards. They told me they wanted to sit together, set good intentions, and invite the magic in. So we got magazines, ordered vision board kits on Amazon, and we sat together on New Year's Day and dreamed. It was really cool to watch them create their vision for the year ahead and witness their deep belief that they could make it happen.

The two of them have been super excited as I've been writing this book. They're so happy we're sharing our belief in making things magical and are so proud of me. It has truly touched my heart. Having them be in the photos, helping me pick decorations to share, and allowing me to read them things as I write has been one of the most special things I've ever created. It's been our creation as a family: Brian, Atticus, Autumn, Aidan, and me. We all signed up to believe in this life being magical and we really work to make that happen as much as possible. It's the little things that make big magic.

Magical Thoughts on Mother's Day

I was really thinking about Mother's Day this year. I was remembering all the brunches, flowers, cards, and Mother's Day moments I had with my mom before she passed, and I realized this: my mom was grateful for every flower, brunch, card, and moment on that day every year, but I think what she really wanted was to see and feel that all she gave to me as a mom mattered. She wanted to share stories with me about who she was and have me listen. She wanted to give me advice and then watch me apply it and have it help. She wanted me to not roll my eyes every time she asked for one more hug or kiss. She wanted me to just once understand all it took to make that birthday party or holiday really magical. She didn't want me to challenge her every time she had to be tough or set rules. She wanted me to say thank you. Not for things, but for her time. For her willingness to do at any given moment what needed to be done for me, for me to be okay, and for my life to be even a little bit better or easier than the moment before.

Mother's Day is weird. Sometimes because I feel bad making my family celebrate me as a mom. So I like to make it a day more about how lucky I feel to be a mom and how lucky we are to have each other. But as a mom myself, I do now wish at those brunches that I would've said how much I appreciated her. How much I witnessed her do. How deeply her love made a difference in my every day. I wish I would've never rolled my eyes, and hugged her tighter and kissed her more instead. I can only hope she felt seen by me even once.

So, to all the moms . . . I see you. Being a mom is everything, and everything is also a lot to carry. Spoil your moms if you have them, send cheers to your moms in heaven so they can hear you, and be kind to a mom around you because you never know what she is going through. Make sure your moms know they matter. Not just on Mother's Day but every day.

The Entertaining Mommy

I had heard about the mom stereotypes: yoga mom, glam mom, helicopter mom. They all sounded daunting. Besides the fact that we shouldn't stereotype each other, it was scary thinking about where I would fit in. What label would I fall under as a new mom? I had only been an entertainer my whole life. How would that help me? What had a life as an entertainer prepared me for in motherhood?

After months of late-night breastfeeding, trying to help a new human sleep, long days of silly faces, and making a new schedule for our family so we could thrive, that's when it hit me! I found my true mom self at 2 am under a pile of breast milk bags. I was the *entertaining mommy*. They say life is what prepares you for motherhood—well, *they*, whoever *they* are, were right. Time went by and we added another baby only eighteen months later. It was then that I realized I had the opportunity to introduce the old entertainer me to the new mommy me, and they could work together.

Long hours of night shoots had gotten me ready for nighttime feedings and no sleep in those first months of newborns. The unpredictable set days, where everything needs to shift and you need to shift with it while keeping your cool, was just like riding the tides of a toddler's moods. Doing a one-hour drama for years, where you truly don't remember what being rested feels like, was so far just like my experience of having two kids eighteen months apart. Directing the household through doctor appointments, playdates, gym class, dance class, and Mommy and Me classes was like directing a show, sticking to your shooting schedule, and bringing the day in quick, stress-free, and with the crew happy.

You get the point. I wasn't *playing* a mom; I *was* a mom. The entertaining doesn't stop, by the way. At any given moment you have to be ready with a joke, story, song, funny face, dance routine, iPad, or clown nose (yes, I have one in my purse). And don't get me started on playdates! I also became a casting director, trying to find the perfect cast for a playful and fun time, learning how to avoid a temperamental lead and a feisty day player. Although I don't think we should label each other, being known as the entertaining mommy feels good. Everything I was before being a mom has helped me and it has felt incredible to find that. So, my advice: when life throws big changes your way, take the old you and the new you and create the *now* you.

Writing Prompt

Who made magic in your life? What does creating magic in your life look like? You can now use this as an inspiration place to remember you are magical.

_____

_____

_____

_____

_____

_____

_____

_____

_____

_____

_____

♥ This window has been a place of magic from the day we moved in. The kids look for Santa in that window and at our big tree wrapped in holiday lights every year. We have talked to the man in the moon from that window and I have made a wish or two out to the universe while looking out this window. It's our magic place.

2.
EVERYDAY MAGIC

"Find the magic in the everyday moments. The small things. The things that at times you brush off or move through quickly. Because they seem boring or mundane. They seem so small that they're not worth thinking about, nor remembering. But as time passes and you look back at life, those will be the things that hold the most magic. Those little things will be what you crave more of. Those everyday things will be what warms your heart. This is your reminder to enjoy them today. To look for them, love them, and treasure them. The small things really do become the big things."

LISA BUSCOMB
@WORDS_BY_WILDE_ROAD

I understand that the idea of everyday magic can sound like an other thing you have to find time for in your day. But it's not,

I promise. It's all about the prep: ordering ahead of time, getting creative, and using your heart. The world will teach our kids about heartbreak, failures, unkind people, and harsh realities. For me, I want our home to feel like magic is all around us. We still have real conversations and understand the truth of the world, but at any given moment to soften the blow or just to smile a little extra we make magic. Trust me, as a grown-up and a parent, making the magic does a world of good for my heart and spirit as well. So here are some ideas from our family to yours.

Mommy Magic 101

Okay, my kind of magic needs no candle, cauldron, perfect moon, or book. (Except this book, of course.) My magic is your magic. It doesn't come from a spell. It comes from your heart. It's making the ordinary a little extra because the extra is magical. I realize that it can be hard to think of ideas on your own. So I always pull inspiration from fellow magic-makers. Pinterest, Instagram, and Etsy are full of magical moms doing extra special things and adding extra special touches to help us be creative and fun. Companies like Glitterville (my magical guru), Bonjour Fête, Ellie and Piper, and Meri Meri are always providing party ideas and themes, but are also my go-to places for decorations and party needs. It's okay to think, "Ugh, I can't take on any more. This sounds like a lot." I still feel that way sometimes, but I promise taking a deep breath, making a plan, placing the orders, and then creating the magic will be worth it when your kids have the best time ever. My kids' friends think I'm extra for sure, but they always want to come to our parties and gatherings, because they say our house has magic, which is honestly the best compliment ever! Mommy magic can also happen in small ways. We have lots of little things we do at our house to keep the magic going even without a birthday or holiday to celebrate. Some of my favorites are . . .

DINNER AROUND THE WORLD

One thing my kids love is something we call Dinner Around the World. So far, their favorite one is Paris. Around dinnertime I told my kids to get dressed up in French fashion and be downstairs at 4:30 pm. When they arrived in Paris (our kitchen), the table was decorated with fancy plates, napkins, and pink flowers. The sparkling apple cider was served chilled, and I only spoke in my worst French accent. I thought it was good. They weren't convinced, though, and I got a "No, Mommy." Kids are tough critics.

On the menu was steak frites; Siri played "Le Vie En Rose," and I provided some facts about France to sneak in some learning. It was an enchanted evening full of fun and using our imaginations. Whether you plan an Italian dinner of hand-tossed pizzas, matcha mochi from Japan, or even some Indian chicken tikka masala, it's a really fun way to create dinnertime magic and get the kids to try new food. *Oui oui!*

MAGIC CLOSET

A magic closet or drawer is a must! Fill it with the tubs of slime you normally say no to. Add a few silly costumes, Play-Doh,

Autumn was very impressed with how she dressed herself and Atticus for this dinner. Atticus rang the doorbell and picked Autumn up for this date and I was truly impressed with my ability to remain in a French accent. (Terrible but French-ish.)

painting projects, Squishmallows, small Lego sets . . . whatever your kids find magical. When homework is super-challenging, or a random Tuesday or rainy weekend needs a pick-me-up, surprise them! Magic can be anytime and for no reason at all!

MOON WATER

Yes, moon water! This is one of my favorites, and so easy! On the night of a full moon, take a bottle of water and let it sit outside all night taking in the moon's magic. The next morning, ask your kids to set some good intentions for themselves, or write a word

on the bottle as a manifestation like *kindness, fun,* or *abundance.*
Then they have to drink the bottle of water, feeling the moon's
magic and the intention that they set with every sip. It's magical
... and a clever way to get them to drink water!

BASKETS OF JOY

The basket of joy! This one is so fun. It doesn't have to be expensive or big, but a basket of joy is a great way to celebrate all the
things that need some extra magic. I do summer baskets for my
kids to kick off the summer: sunscreen, sunglasses, pool toys, let-
ter kits to keep in touch with friends who travel, memory books
for special summer memories, and balloons for water balloon
fights. These are just some ideas; you can make it your own.

I do back-to-school baskets with pencils, fun markers, folders, and so on. All the school supplies they need, and a few little
surprises like stickers and a new water bottle to decorate. It's a
fun way to say, "Let's get excited for this new school year!" and
it makes saying goodbye to summer a little easier.

We do Valentine's Day boxes filled with valentines to make
for friends, a few sweet treats, a stuffy to squeeze, heart glasses,
or new Valentine's pajamas.

I have also made sick boxes for when my littles are sick. I put
in air-dry clay, snacks, crayons, coloring books, a little get-well-
soon card or note, and, of course, lots of extra love.

One way to use everyday magic is by creating moments for
people you love, moments that are simple and easy but made just
for what they adore. My niece Campbell came to visit over the
summer, and she loves mushrooms. We wanted to make her feel

This brilliant idea came from my Instagram mom friend @homewithjanan. She makes the most amazing baskets for her kids, and now I do also. Magic makers in the world are so special.

extra special when she arrived, so we decided to do a mushroom welcome dinner. I went on Amazon and typed in "mushroom party." So many fun things came up. We made a fun tablescape out of mushroom-themed décor, wore silly mushroom hats, had mushroom plates and napkins, and we went wild with the mushroom theme. It was her special thing and she felt so loved. Again, not fancy. Not hard, but for sure magical. Magic isn't just the *stuff*. It's the thought and prep that makes a normal meal a magical one.

Another silly dose of magic we added to a somewhat normal day was when Autumn got her braces. That's a big day for a kid,

and we wanted her to feel special, celebrated, and of course add a little magic. So my friend Amanda from Dip'd n Drip'd bakery made tooth cake pops and cookies with braces on them. We invited a few friends over to show off Autumn's cool new mouth jewelry and made it a fun celebration. She forgot about her mouth being sore, and instead had fun with her friends and felt really special. These simple little things go a long way in adding everyday magic.

Again, these are my ideas. Take them or make them your own and use them for anything you want to celebrate. Michaels and Target have super fun things that aren't fancy or super expensive and will make your kids smile. The only requirement is your belief in magic. Bipitty boppity boo!

We have this magical rainbow that shows up on one wall in our house and every time it shows up, we run fast to get in it and soak up the colorful magic. These are some of my favorite rainbow pics. (Brian not pictured because he is too tall to get down to the floor and fit into the rainbow.)

Playful Magic

I worried a lot when I was a first-time mommy that the inner child in me who grew up way too quickly, not fully realized, would somehow mess up the mommy part. Sure, I was a kid and did kid things, but I also navigated an adult business, a full-time job, and spent more time at events than playdates. I have never been to a high school party or prom, and my biggest fear has always been, "Will I be able to help my kids through things I didn't experience firsthand?"

I've played characters who went through growing pains at school, but for me, from fourth grade on, being a kid and student was very different from the experience of most kids. My school was in a trailer on the set of whatever project I was working on. And let me say, it was incredible! I would change nothing. But it does give me a parental insecurity that I didn't think of until now.

As I have grown with my kids and into my Momjo (you know, like "mojo" but for a mom), I've realized that my strengths may not be the same as other moms. My strength is my own special thing that allows me and my kids to thrive and feel joy. My strength is play. I can create silly characters when they are grumpy or sick that make them laugh. I can meet them in the world of imagination in a way someone else couldn't. I can help them get through tough times with silly voices, songs, and laughter. The little kid in me has a place to thrive with my kids, and the mom in me feels confidence in the magic we create and enjoy.

So let's talk about playful magic with your kids, how to create fun, and easy little things you can do that make being together more fun. Tap into your inner kid vibe and show your kids you can be an amazing parent but also really silly. They need us to help them remember it's okay to be a silly kid, and to hold on to that as long as possible in a world that moves so fast.

Creating five days of not-your-average dinner is a great way to open up a magical portal of family silly time and sends a clear signal to that coming weekend that you are ready for some fun. Here are some dinner ideas to awaken your inner child and tell your kids that it's time to play!

THE LET IT GLOW DINNER

Search "glow-in-the-dark party" on Amazon and so many things come up! Glasses, glow sticks, garland, balloons, and glow-in-the-dark plates.

Buy what you can, decorate a space, and let it glow! Maybe it's a good Friday night activity to say, "The week is over. Let's have some fun." I would order pizza for this, because it's easy to eat in the dark. Don't stop just with dinner. Add glow sticks to bath time before bed, place some near toothbrushes, and of course in their bedrooms for a sleepy glow vibe.

YOU INVITED WHO TO DINNER?

This one is a favorite of mine! It's like my favorite murder mystery dinner parties, but kid-friendly. Tell one or more people in your family to create a person who is coming to dinner that night, and become that person complete with details about who they are that they can share at the table. Costumes, wigs, and props are all very much appreciated, and the mystery guest should try to stay in character the whole time. It's silly and makes the average Tuesday feel new and playful.

DINNER AND A SHOW

Okay, set the stage! Cook something delicious, of course, and then put on a family talent show. Brian and I would probably do a song with Brian on guitar and me on vocals. Autumn would do something Taylor Swift. Aidan is really good at telling what animals he sees in his book, and Atticus would either show us soccer moves or dance moves because he is really good at both. Everyone gets a chance to do something they love and feel supported.

BREAKFAST FOR DINNER

This one helps get the bedtime routine started early, because everyone has to show up for dinnertime in pajamas. Only breakfast foods are served, and if you dare . . . serve it in bed. If not, just at the table is fun. Pick out a movie everyone enjoys, snuggle up under blankets, and enjoy your happy kids.

CRAZY TACO TUESDAY!

This is one that Autumn created. It's like Taco Tuesday, but not your normal taco. Make a silly food bar on your counter with crazy taco fillings: spaghetti, sour gummi worms, chicken fingers, bacon, eggs, pepperoni, cheese, whatever seems edible but weird, and let everyone create a crazy taco! Then sit down and play Taco Versus Burrito, one of our favorite silly games to play.

Breakfast for dinner started as anything I could think of to get my kids to eat. The struggle is real, but putting all of their favorite things on this big, beautiful board and making it feel fun and exciting got them to eat up with joy. I highly recommend a board, so your kids don't get bored.

ONE COLOR ONLY

This dinner is another Autumn creation. It is what it sounds like. Let everyone agree on a color. Easier said than done, but once you pick your color and décor, build your menu around that. Have everyone wear the chosen color to dinner!

PARENTS' NIGHT OFF

This one might just be impossible, if I'm being honest. But if you can make it happen, it's one of my favorites. It can seem scary, but the kids will love it. For one night, your kids have to decide what they want to eat and either cook it (with assistance, of course) or order in. Let them design a menu. You get all the ingredients and make the food, except leave the chopping for the kids and give stove or oven assistance. Let them set the table, and you arrive at whatever restaurant they have created and play along. Eat the food, if you dare, and let them giggle and feel proud of what they have made for the family. They also have to clean up! Things we as parents can't do: 1) judge how messy they make the kitchen or 2) decide what they eat. We have to be loving and supportive and enjoy the one night off, while spending time with them and seeing what choices they make. Your kids might surprise you!

These are just a few of my ideas. Make up new ones, change these to fit your family better, but add some magical play into your week. The important point is that we don't need a reason to play with our kids. Playing with them can mean sports, board games, crafts, imagination adventures, scavenger hunts, snuggles, and movie time. It just means it's time to remember the kid in you, and let that kid spend time with them. Escape all the pressure for a moment and just be in the fun.

The Magical Dinners User Guide

Here are a few ideas to make the lull of the work/school week a little bit more exciting for both you and your kids. I call them . . . magical dinners. Get your dinner ideas and anything you need prepped and ready ahead of time. Decide on the week, one where you can fully commit. Obviously this isn't a week when the kids have big tests, when you have tons of extra work on your plate, or when anything else stressful is going on that would take away from the fun mindset. Parents, I know dinnertime is already crazy, and you may think I'm nuts for making it more complicated. But remember that this is as much for you as them, if not more. Time goes by so fast. While they still want to eat dinner with you, why not take one week and make it special? And if it's a hit, maybe plan one week of magic dinners per month? Or every other month?

1. Once you've chosen your week, decide which days will work best for which dinners.
2. Label some envelopes, one per dinner, with the day and date of each so you know what's coming.
3. Place instructions, or a mini write-up about what the dinner will be, in each envelope. If you're feeling creative, add pictures from the internet that go with each day's theme.
4. Let the kids know on Sunday that the following week is

going to get magical and weird! Share each envelope before dinner, then watch as the magic unfolds! What happens next is bonding with your kids, some silly moments, and memories made!

Birthday Magic

When I started hearing about birthday parties for kids, it was a lot to take in. Vendors, themes, gift bags, and over-the-top ideas that only seem to get bigger every year. It felt not only expensive, but truly like a world I wasn't prepared for. Those were not the birthday parties of my childhood. Instead of staying in a state of overwhelm, I decided that I would put my inner magic-maker to work and create what would feel magical to my kids. Some of their parties have been bigger, and some not as much. I've learned to spend my budget on the stuff I can't do myself, create the things I can in an easy and inexpensive way, and still crush the party vibes for your kids and guests.

My mom was amazing at birthdays! When I was a kid, it was the simple things like Chuck E. Cheese and the best store-bought birthday cake. But I remember, even at a young age, my mom truly making me feel that the day I was born was special, every year. And not just mine—she loved to celebrate birthdays in general. When I was young, I loved to skate at the roller skating rink, and this very cute older boy, maybe twelve or thirteen, would drive around whoever was celebrating a birthday in a giant roller skate car. You got to pick your favorite song and it was three minutes of bliss. I waited so long for my chance, and when my

turn came, I remember thinking at that moment, "Wow, birthdays are so cool!"

The magic was always in the details. Not every party was huge, but each birthday felt tailored, with special touches toward who you were that year. One of the most special birthdays was my thirtieth, thanks to my mom. I have always loved Audrey

Hepburn, so my mom threw me a *Breakfast at Tiffany's* party. We started that morning actually having breakfast in Tiffany's, with a few friends, family, my mom, and grandma. It was incredible. Coffee, croissants, and sparkly diamonds! Then we had afternoon tea, and a big party that night with a Tiffany's box cake. It was truly so special, all in the details.

When I had my babies and started looking around at all the parties people threw for their kids, it was daunting. I really didn't know if I could do the creative things I was seeing, or spend what it looked like you had to spend, for a kid's party to be special for *every* birthday. Then I remembered that not every party I had was over the top and extravagant (some totally were), but what I remembered the most and took with me were the little details that made it special. So, I decided that for *my* kids' parties, that's where I would start. Gift bags are a great place to show creativity, fun, and add special touches. The week before the party, I pre-make gift bags, and then set them out with the décor, to get as much ready in advance as possible. That way, on the day of the event, you can put it all out quickly, get ready, and make spending time with your kid the priority.

Three successful tips for birthday magic:

1. Choose a theme
2. Get your kids' ideas
3. Decide how much money to spend on your magic

STEP 1: The biggest thing that helps me in planning these parties is having a clear theme! Once you have a theme, you can go Pinterest and Insta crazy, looking at what others have done,

After being able to play Audrey Hepburn in a movie, a *Breakfast at Tiffany's*-themed 30th birthday party seemed perfect for my special day. My mom planned everything and told me nothing. The day was filled with so many amazing moments. I felt so loved and my mom was truly in her best magic-making mode for this one!

making it your own, getting inspiration, and then making it all work for your budget.

STEP 2: Make it fun for your kids and get them involved. See what your kids are most interested in and pull from that. If it's Super Mario, watch the *Super Mario* movie and let them tell you what they love most, and then incorporate that into the activities or decorations. Google Paris and learn about it; Autumn wanted berets, French pastries, and a caricature artist, so we did that and then built the party around it. For Aidan, well, he loves Hot Wheels, so we just did a cute party built around his love of cars.

I would also take the time to enjoy it when your kids are super little and you can take control. As they get older, lots of changing opinions and changing minds come into play. It's so fun as they get older, but a little harder to nail down the details.

STEP 3: Now that you have some details in mind, figure out what you want to spend most of your money on. Props? Cake? Gift bags? The rest you can fill in and make cute with what's left in your budget.

When I think back on all of my birthday parties, I never think of how much was spent on them, or which ones were elaborate and which ones were simple. I just remember feeling special, loving my birthday, and feeling like the day I was born was really cool and worth celebrating. The parties we all see on social media (mine included) aren't accomplishments to emulate. They should inspire, and maybe help you think of something you wouldn't normally do on your own. The birthday magic is what comes from you for your kids or loved ones, from your heart. Go make magic!

Birthday Party #1: Oui Oui Party

It can be hard for kids to stay focused on a party theme, though I think because my littles are part Holiday Junkie (thanks to me) they seem to do great at it. Halloween costumes are a whole other story—they change costume ideas twenty-five times until the big day. But my kids are clear and precise with what they want as a party theme. So that's helpful.

For Autumn's ninth birthday, she knew exactly what she wanted. Since she was born, she has been drawn to Paris. She was actually in Paris once, while in my belly. The city still speaks to her, and she wants to go there one day. So, when we said, "Um, not this year," she countered with some very convincing reasons on why we should fly her to Paris for her ninth birthday. The reasons had a lot to do with desserts. They *all* had to do with dessert, so we decided a Oui Oui birthday party it would be.

Autumn wanted an Eiffel Tower, macarons, a poodle (if possible), berets for everyone . . . and to make Paris-themed slime. So I went to work. Where we live, we're very lucky to have really cool companies around to help bring things to life. But other than the slime setup and Parisian props, the rest of what we needed was available via Etsy, Amazon, and a French bakery! Let me break it down.

I went straight to Amazon for berets and Eiffel Tower bubble bottles for gift bags.

Bonjour Fête had macaron erasers that were cute for gift bags as well.

Speaking of gift bags, they had to be extra special. I found this

amazing woman on Etsy whose company is Gilda's Curated Designs. The bags were spectacular and not expensive at all.

Our amazing friend at the bakery Maison Macha made all the French treats for the kids.

Platinum Prop House, the prop rental company that I use for most of our parties, had an Eiffel Tower available, as well as Parisian letters, a pink poodle, a flower wall, and a French dessert cart! I highly recommend seeing if you have a prop house in your area. It opens up so many possibilities for parties and events, since they often have a bigger variety of options than typical party rental places.

A place called Little Artist Party does amazing kid slime experiences. So, we decided pink slime would be cool with Parisian charms. You can also find great slime tutorials and recipes on Pinterest to make your own slime, and get charms on Amazon if you don't have a place that can do it for you.

The last thing we thought of was a caricature artist who could draw Autumn and her friends like the artists on the streets of Paris. I did some online searching and found someone, and she was amazing! The kids loved their portraits as take-home party favors.

Oh, and for balloons, we ordered balloons that floated around the party in pastel macaron colors from event stylist The Balloon Cart. That was Autumn's idea. The party was a blast. After the props were set up and gift bags were filled, the rest was easy. The kids loved it! *C'est Magnifique!*

Birthday Party #2: Super Atticus

The Mario party for Atticus has been one of my favorites! He wanted all things Mario, of course. But I wanted to throw a very special party that was more about Atticus than Mario. So, it started with changing the party name from Super Mario to Super Atticus.

I had to really tailor the day to my sweet boy and what he loves. I reached out again to my friends at Platinum Prop House. They went to work on checking for what they had as backdrop possibilities, and then they made an incredible sign that said "Super Atticus," which now hangs in his room.

I found boxes for the table centerpieces on Etsy, and had them customized with "Super Atticus" printed on them. My kids are creative and crafty, so my friends at Little Artist Party came up with the idea of providing little clay/dough "Mario Land" kits that the kids could make and put together.

Atticus doesn't like cake but loves ice cream, so I called Gourmeletas and decided to book an ice cream cart. It's perfect for a summer birthday when it's hot, and it's not cake! They took the art from the backdrop and put it on the cart, so it became a Super Atticus (ice cream) Kart! I was proud of that one!

Because I wanted to keep the big kids busy (it's better for everyone when they are busy), I searched on Google and found a game truck rental. They parked a truck, basically a video arcade on wheels, right in front of our driveway, and the kids got to play Mario video games for hours. It was so awesome! We had the game truck running from 10:30 am to 12:30 pm while the parents

all hung out in the backyard, then the kids came to the backyard for crafts and ice cream. It was perfect.

I kept the gift bags simple, with tons of Mario stuff in cute bags I found on Etsy. The kids were so happy, and months later Atticus still says it was his best party yet! Of course he has already started talking about next year's party, but this mama needs a break first!

Birthday Party #3: Two Fast

For Aidan, we've only had two birthdays so far, and I can't wait to get into more fun planning for him and seeing what he loves! For his first birthday we planned a farm party, because he loves animals. And this year we went hot and heavy on the "2 Fast" theme, because our little man loves his Hot Wheels!

Backdrops, as you can see from our parties, are very important to me. I love to have a great photo op place for kids and parents, so I knew we needed a finish line setup for photos. Platinum Prop House made it look amazing. Aidan loved it, and had the best time climbing up on the numbered podium. The rest was easy, because he's still so little. I ordered five Hot Wheels tracks, and made them birthday presents he could open. Atticus is amazing at setting those up, so he was my track guy!

I bought toy cars in bulk and put them into easy grab baskets for the kids, and found cute street mats to put under the tracks, so it looked extra fun. Shavs Paper designed a custom paper that I ended up using to decorate a gift area. It was so cute. I ordered all the gift swag off of Amazon, and even the cute bags. It wasn't fancy but so fun, so cute, and designed with special thought for our little man. I send out invitations early because parents appreciate being able to schedule in advance. It also gives you the best shot of having all your kids' friends be able to join in the fun.

Aidan's favorite food is pancakes, so we had a pancake artist making pancakes as a special touch and the kids loved it. It was a super-special party and Aidan, and our big kids, had a lot of fun. I can't wait to see what he is into by next year!

Aidan will of course only remember his 1st birthday by seeing the pics someday, but for us it was important to celebrate and have fun with our friends and for our big kids to feel special also. He has loved animals from the day he was born. @littlehorseontheprairie brought all the animals. It was our little animal lover's dream come true.

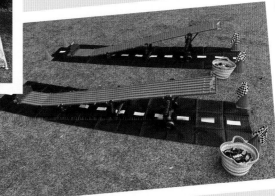

Spideycus is our nickname for Atticus. He has always been a Spider-Man lover. He was so excited for this Spidey-themed party, and we had the best day! We did web-inspired cotton candy, a bounce house, and lots of superhero fun!

These are some more fun ideas to get your magic wheels turning for your own special birthday parties! Make memories and add some magic!

Writing Prompt

I've told you how we create everyday magic, now it's time to make it your own. Write some ideas for you and your family.

_____

_____

_____

_____

_____

_____

_____

_____

_____

_____

_____

_____

_____

_____

_____

3.
RECIPE
MAGIC

After my grandmother and my mom passed, the two most important women in my life, I remember looking through boxes of memories hoping for anything with their handwriting on it. You don't realize how important handwritten notes, recipes, and saved messages mean until they are all you have left to hold on to.

I reached out to my aunt for recipes from my grandmother, and I have a book my sister-in-law and brother gave me with my mom's recipes in it. It's one of my greatest treasures. I added a funny recipe my brother had given me, and asked my two sisters-in-law, who love to cook, for recipes they love making. Brian's mom gave me recipes from her mom that are special, and it wouldn't be Christmas for us without Brian's famous Christmas Eve pasta recipe.

Some of our greatest memories in life are over shared meals and laughter, or moments cooking with our grandmothers, moms, spouses, and kids in the kitchen. Cooking is something that Autumn and Atticus love to do with Nana (Brian's mom) when she is in town, and that I loved to do with my G-ma when she would visit. It seems only fitting, in this book of sharing my family stories, that I also give you some of the recipes that I hold dear. All of these have a special place in my heart, and I hope if you try them, they find a place in yours. Note that some of these passed-along recipes have never been written down before, so you may have to work out a few of the minor details yourself. Which is another way of saying, you can experiment and make them your own!

G-MA'S CHICKEN AND DUMPLINGS

FOR THE STEW:

1 whole chicken cut into pieces (the butcher can do this, or you can buy it already packaged like this)

6 cups water or low-sodium chicken broth

1 small onion, chopped fine

1 medium carrot, peeled and cut into ½-inch pieces (optional)

2 celery ribs, chopped fine

1 bag frozen peas (optional)

1 teaspoon fresh thyme (optional)

¼ cup chopped fresh parsley (optional)

Salt, to taste

Freshly ground pepper, to taste

FOR THE DUMPLINGS:

Box of Bisquick

Add the chicken to a heavy stock pot or Dutch oven and cover with water or broth. Cover and cook over medium heat for 30 minutes. Remove chicken and set aside to cool.

Meanwhile, make the dumplings according to the Bisquick recipe on the box (for regular biscuits). Roll them very thin, about ⅛- to ¼-inch thick. Cut into 2-inch squares and leave exposed to the air to dry out a bit.

Once the chicken is cooked and removed from the stock, add onion, carrots (if using), celery, and peas (if using) to the pot. Turn up the heat to high and bring to a boil. Reduce heat and cook for 10 to 15 minutes, or until the vegetables are just tender.

While the vegetables are cooking, remove the chicken meat from the bones and discard the skin and fat. Shred the meat and set aside.

Add the dried-out dumplings to the stock pot a few at a time (make sure not to crowd them) until there is a layer across the top of the stew. Cover the pan and let them cook for 3 to 5 minutes or until a toothpick inserted in the middle comes out clean. (The cooking time could be much longer. Grandma wasn't very specific about the time, so the toothpick test should help.) Season with salt and pepper and serve.

G-MA SHIPP'S SUGAR COOKIES

2 cups flour

1 teaspoon cream of tartar

½ teaspoon baking soda

½ teaspoon salt

¾ cup granulated sugar

½ cup melted shortening (or butter)

2 eggs

1 teaspoon vanilla

Sift the flour, cream of tartar, baking soda, and salt in a bowl. Measure the sugar into a large bowl and add shortening. Break the eggs into a small bowl and beat well. Add to the shortening/sugar mixture. Stir in the vanilla and gradually add flour mixture. Form into a ball and refrigerate for at least 3 hours.

Roll out in sections, keeping the extra dough cold. Don't overwork the dough. Cut into shapes and bake on a greased cookie sheet at 350°F until lightly brown. Keep a close eye on them so they don't overcook. Remove and let cool on a rack before decorating with colored icing and sprinkles.

NOTE: You can substitute 2 teaspoons baking powder for cream of tartar and baking soda.

HEWITT-STYLE CREAM CHEESE PIE

1 8-oz. package cream cheese, softened
1 can Eagle brand sweetened condensed milk
¼ cup juice from 1 lemon
Lemon zest (optional)
1 store-bought graham cracker crust

In the bowl of a standing mixer fitted with the paddle attachment (or with a hand mixer, or a spoon and good old-fashioned elbow grease), cream the cream cheese until smooth. Add the sweetened condensed milk, lemon juice, and zest (if using) until smooth and combined.

Pour the mixture into the pie shell.

Refrigerate for a minimum of 4 hours.

To serve: leave it plain or top with the fruit of your choice.

MY MOM'S WHITE BEAN CHICKEN CHILI

2 to 3 large chicken breasts, bone-in
2 stalks celery
1 onion, skin removed and cut in half
Water to cover chicken
1 small package white beans
½ cup celery, diced
½ cup carrots, diced
1 cup onion, diced
1 teaspoon ground cumin
1 teaspoon oregano
¼ teaspoon cayenne pepper (optional)
Salt and freshly ground pepper to taste
1 can Ro-Tel diced tomatoes and chilies (blend of your choice)

Place chicken, celery, and onion in a stock pot and add enough water to just cover. Boil chicken until just barely cooked (otherwise it becomes tough). Remove chicken and set aside to cool. Strain stock through a sieve into a large bowl. Discard solids. Remove chicken from bones and shred. Set aside.

Add stock and a bag of small white beans to the stock pot and simmer until beans are tender, about 1½ hours. Add celery, carrots, onion, chicken, cumin, oregano, cayenne pepper (if using), and salt and freshly ground pepper to taste. Bring to a boil, reduce heat, and simmer 20 to 30 minutes. Finally, add the Ro-Tel (if added too soon, the tomatoes will stop the beans from cooking and getting tender) and cook another 15 minutes. Taste and adjust seasonings.

NANA'S APPLE PIE

Pie crust (double)

6 large apples, sliced very thinly

1 tablespoon lemon juice (lemon zest optional)

⅛ teaspoon nutmeg

1½ teaspoons cinnamon

½ cup white sugar

½ cup brown sugar

¼ teaspoon salt

2 tablespoons flour

1 teaspoon vanilla extract

2 tablespoons unsalted butter

White egg wash or milk for top crust

Cut apple slices thin. Put in a bowl with a little lemon juice (to keep from turning).

Mix the nutmeg, cinnamon, white sugar, brown sugar, salt, flour, and vanilla, then add the apples and coat them well.

Roll out the pie crust and lay it in the pie pan. Add apple ingredients to the pie pan. Cut 2 tablespoons of butter into small pieces and put on top of the apples.

Roll out the second crust thin, and lay it on top of the apples. Connect the top and bottom crust together with your fingers. Flute the edges. Prick fork holes on top. Make a white egg wash, and with a pastry brush put it on the top pie crust. Add a little more sugar to the top.

Preheat the oven to 425°F and bake for 20 minutes. Then reduce to 350°F and bake for 25 minutes more or until the crust is golden and the apples are tender.

NANA'S MANICOTTI

FOR THE CREPES:

1 cup semolina or all-purpose
   flour
Salt
1 egg
1 cup club soda
Olive oil to coat pan

FOR THE FILLING:

1 15-oz. container ricotta

12 oz. mozzarella shredded
   cheese
¾ cup grated Parmesan cheese
1 egg
Parsley
Salt and pepper
Pasta sauce of your choice
More Parmesan and mozzarella
   for topping

Add all the crepe ingredients together, mix well. Add more club soda to get mix thinner.

Heat a 6" frying pan with a little olive oil. I spread the oil on with paper towels so it's just lightly coated.

When the pan is hot (medium heat), add a little of the crepe mix and tilt the pan so the mix coats the whole pan. Set it on the burner for 1 minute, then flip it for 30 seconds more.

Remove the crepe from the pan. Lay it on parchment paper. Repeat for the next crepe, adding more olive oil to the pan if necessary. If the batter seems too thick, thin it with more club soda. Mix often. Repeat until the batter is done, yielding 10–15 crepes (depending on the thickness of the batter).

Mix the filling ingredients together in a small bowl until well blended.

Lay the crepes out. Add a large spoonful of filling to each. Mix it to the middle of the crepe, and fold over one side to make the crepe roll.

Put pasta sauce on 9 x 12 glass baking dish. Lay the crepes down in the dish, side by side, folded sides down. Add more sauce on top. Add mozzarella cheese and Parmesan cheese.

Cover with foil and bake at 350°F for 30 minutes. (Cheese can also be melted in the microwave and added after baking.)

BRIAN'S BUCATINI AMATRICIANA

9–12 oz. guanciale (pork cheek)
Olive oil
1 large white onion
1 peperoncino (dry red Italian hot pepper), crushed
1 28-oz. can crushed San Marzano tomatoes
1 28-oz. can pureed San Marzano tomatoes
1 tube tomato paste
Black pepper
Powdered Pecorino Romano cheese to taste
Salt to taste
1 lb. bucatini pasta

Slice the guanciale into matchstick-sized slices. Heat some oil in a pan. When hot, add the guanciale. Cook over medium-high heat until golden and crunchy.

Remove the guanciale from the pan with a slotted spoon and set aside, keeping it warm. Leave the rendered fat (oil) in the pan but remove from heat. If it doesn't look like you have enough oil to cook the onion, add some olive oil. Slice the onions length-wise (julienne), and after putting the pan back onto the heat, add onions to the pan with the oil and the fat from the guanciale.

Add the crushed peperoncino. When the onions are slightly translucent (about 5 minutes), add the cans of tomatoes and cook until reduced some, but not too thin. Add some of the to-mato paste, to taste, and some black pepper. Turn off the heat and add about half of the Pecorino; mix well. Taste and add salt and more black pepper if necessary.

Cook the bucatini as instructed for al dente. Drain the buca-tini and mix in the sauce. Add the crunchy guanciale and mix it all together. Serve immediately with the leftover Pecorino cheese sprinkled on top of each plate.

TODD'S I PUT THE *T* IN TATER TOT CASSEROLE

1–2 lbs. extra-lean ground meat

1 bag frozen mixed vegetables (peas, corn, carrots)

1 bag frozen broccoli

1 can cream of mushroom soup

1 can cream of broccoli soup

1 bag frozen tater tots

Seasonings to taste

Brown the ground meat. Add/mix in the frozen mixed vegetables, broccoli, and soups. Season to taste.

Add the mix to a baking or casserole dish. Layer top with tater tots.

Bake at 375°F for approximately 35 minutes.

Remove from oven, sprinkle with shredded cheddar cheese, and let stand for 5 minutes.

Serve with cold beer and elastic waistband.

MICHELLE'S BOLOGNESE LASAGNA

FOR THE BOLOGNESE FILLING:

2 peeled carrots

½ onion

2–4 cloves of garlic

8 oz. mushrooms (optional)

4 tablespoons unsalted butter

1 28-oz. can whole San Marzano tomatoes

1½ lbs. ground meat (any kind will work; I prefer beef)

1½ cups milk

1½ cups wine (white or red, one you like to drink)

1–2 tablespoons tomato paste (to your taste)

½ teaspoon sugar (balances the acidity in the tomatoes)

1–2 tablespoons kosher salt

Ground pepper

Red pepper flakes (optional and to taste)

1–2 teaspoons Aceto Balsamico Essenza, without vinegar (optional)

FOR THE BÉCHAMEL SAUCE AND LASAGNA:

4 tablespoons butter

4 tablespoons all-purpose flour

4 cups milk (whole preferred)

1 package lasagna noodles

2 cups grated Parmesan and mozzarella (or any cheese you prefer)

TO PREPARE THE BOLOGNESE FILLING:

In a food processor, mince the peeled carrots, onions, garlic, and mushrooms (if using). Add the butter to a deep saucepan or cast enamel Dutch oven (my preference) over medium heat. Once melted, add the minced vegetables and cook down until most liquid is evaporated, 5 or so minutes.

While the vegetables cook, add the whole tomatoes and their juice to the same bowl in the food processor and puree as smoothly as you prefer, then set aside. Add the ground meat to the cooking vegetables and cook for about 4–5 minutes, breaking the mixture up into small pieces.

Add the milk and cook until almost all the liquid is absorbed. Then, add the wine and cook until all the liquid is absorbed, continuing to break up the ground meat.

Once all the liquid is absorbed, add the tomato paste and cook through for 1–2 minutes. Add the puréed tomatoes, ½ teaspoon sugar, 1 tablespoon salt or more to taste, ground pepper, and red pepper flakes (optional). If using the Aceto Balsamico (not balsamic vinegar), drizzle over the sauce and stir in, then continue to cook over medium to low heat until the mixture is bubbly and reduced down a bit. Cover partially with lid to help prevent splatters.

TO MAKE THE BÉCHAMEL SAUCE AND LASAGNA:

Heat oven to 375°F.

Melt the butter in a saucepan. Add the flour and whisk for 1–2 minutes to cook the flour. Slowly add the milk, whisking continuously until no lumps remain. Continue cooking until the resulting béchamel sauce remains on the back of a spoon. Test by dipping in a spoon and running your finger along the back. You should be able to draw a line through the sauce on the back of the spoon.

For the lasagna, take a small ladle of the Bolognese filling and spread it on the bottom of a 9 x 13 ceramic dish or disposable aluminum pan. Add a layer of lasagna noodles. Spread 1½ cups Bolognese filling over the noodles, then ladle 1 cup of the béchamel over it. Sprinkle a thin layer of cheese and repeat. End with a thicker layer of cheese on top.

Cover the lasagna tightly with aluminum foil. You can spray the foil with cooking oil before covering the dish to prevent the cheese from sticking.

Bake in the oven for 30 minutes at 375°F. Increase the oven to 425°F and remove the foil, then continue to bake, uncovered, for another 15 minutes or until bubbly and slightly brown on top.

MEG'S DARK CHOCOLATE OATMEAL COOKIES

2½ cups old-fashioned whole rolled oats (not instant)
2 cups all-purpose flour
1 teaspoon baking soda
1 teaspoon baking powder
¾ teaspoon salt
½ teaspoon cream of tartar
1 cup (2 sticks) unsalted butter, at room temperature

1 cup granulated sugar
1 cup firmly packed light brown sugar
2 eggs
1½ teaspoons vanilla extract
16 oz. dark chocolate chips (feel free to add more)

Preheat the oven to 375°F. Line a baking sheet with parchment paper.

Blend the oats in a blender to a fine powder. In a bowl mix together the blended oats, flour, baking soda, baking powder, salt, and cream of tartar. Set aside.

In the bowl of your standing mixer, beat together the butter, granulated sugar, and brown sugar until fluffy (about 3 minutes). Beat in the eggs one at a time. Scrape down the sides, making sure everything is combined. Beat in the vanilla extract. With the mixer on a low speed, gradually add in the flour mixture, beating just until incorporated. With a spatula, fold in the dark chocolate chips.

Use a large cookie scoop to scoop the cookie dough and place the scoops about 2 inches apart on the prepared baking sheet. Bake for 12 minutes. Cookies should be set on the outside, but still look undone in the middle. They will finish setting after being removed from the oven. Let them cool for 3 minutes on the baking sheet, then transfer to a cooling rack to cool completely. Store in an airtight container. (To help the cookies stay soft, toss in a piece of bread when storing them!)

 ## Let's Toast to the Holidays!

One way to have fun with family or friends during the holidays is to add in a bit of festive flair wherever you can! If having friends over or a family dinner, I think naming your cocktails or mocktails is cute and cheery. So here are some ideas I found online for fun twists on some of your basic cocktails. Of course, use your own great ideas and make your own favorites. But remember that simply giving something a festive name sprinkles a little bit of magic on top.

Happy Holidays!

 For the Grown-Ups

BRIAN'S CHRISTMAS COCKTAIL

1½ oz. Angel's Envy Finished Rye   1 oz. Carpano Antica vermouth
1 oz. Gran Classico   Luxardo cherry

Combine liquids in a cocktail shaker. Top with cherry before serving.

THE SANTA CLAUSMOPOLITAN

Lime wedge, for rim
White sanding sugar
Ice
1 cup vodka

½ cup cranberry juice
¼ cup triple sec
¼ cup fresh lime juice
½ cup fresh cranberries

Run a lime wedge around the rims of 4 glasses, then dip each rim in sanding sugar.

Fill a cocktail shaker with ice, then add vodka, cranberry juice, triple sec, and lime juice. Shake until the cocktail shaker is cold.

Divide among the rimmed glasses and add cranberries to each for garnish.

Toast and sip!

THE WITCHY WHISKEY SOUR

4 oz. of your favorite whiskey
 (I do Buffalo Trace)
2 oz. pomegranate juice
 (to create the deep red
 magical potion)
1 tablespoon grenadine syrup

2 oz. freshly squeezed lemon juice
Ice
Pomegranate seeds, for garnish
Orange peel, for garnish

Super simple! Place all of the ingredients into the cocktail shaker with ice (except for the pomegranate seeds and orange peel) and shake for 30 seconds. Strain into glasses with fresh ice. Garnish with pomegranate seeds and twist of orange peel.

 For the Kiddos

HO HO HOT CHOCOLATE

FOR THE HOT CHOCOLATE:
3 cups milk
1 cup cream
¼ cup unsweetened cocoa
    powder
4 tablespoons pure maple syrup
½ cup chocolate chips
¼ teaspoon vanilla extract
Cinnamon to sprinkle

FOR THE MARSHMALLOW SNOWMAN:
Extra-long toothpicks (4 inches)
Marshmallows
Candy corn
Mini chocolate chips
Pretzel sticks

TO MAKE THE HOT CHOCOLATE:
In a small saucepan, add milk, cream, cocoa powder, and maple syrup. Heat over medium heat, whisking frequently until warm.

Add the chocolate chips and vanilla. Whisk until the chocolate is melted and the mixture is creamy. Remove from heat and add in more vanilla. Sprinkle with cinnamon. Serve warm.

TO MAKE THE MARSHMALLOW SNOWMAN:

Take a 4-inch toothpick and place 3 large marshmallows on top of each other.

Then take another toothpick and poke holes in the top marshmallow, making a small opening for a mouth where one piece of candy corn will go. Place the candy corn piece in the opening.

Next, poke two holes in the center of the middle marshmallow, and one on the upper part of the bottom marshmallow, for buttons. Place the mini chocolate chips in those holes.

Poke two holes for arms in the sides of the middle marshmallow, and place a pretzel stick in each of those holes.

Then, poke two holes in the bottom marshmallow for legs and place a pretzel stick in each of those holes.

Place some mini chocolate chips in a sandwich baggie and melt in your microwave (30 seconds at a time until melted). Snip off a tiny corner of the baggie and "pipe" the chocolate out to draw eyes and a mouth on the snowman. Place the marshmallow snowman on top of the hot chocolate, with its arms and legs resting on the cup.

Make sure to let small kids know that there is a toothpick inside the snowman before they start eating it.

VAMPIRE CIDER

1 (25.4-oz.) bottle of sparkling
   apple cider (chilled)
1 liter cranberry ginger ale
   (chilled)
6 cups cranberry juice (chilled)

Juice of 4 limes
Apple wedges
Whole cranberries
Strawberry syrup (for garnish)

In a 4-quart pitcher, pour sparkling apple cider, cranberry ginger ale, cranberry juice, and lime juice over apple wedges and cranberries. Stir gently to combine, adding extra ice if necessary.

Pour strawberry syrup into a condiment bottle and drizzle around the pitcher rim, allowing some to drip down the sides. If desired, garnish chilled glasses to match.

♥ This amazing image was done again by Vanessa Rivera. We call it the Holiday Explosion. It's meant to capture my Holiday Junkie mind and how the kids love being a part of it! We have a big version of this in our house and the kids had so much fun doing the poses and seeing it come together.

4.
THE HOLIDAY JUNKIE

The magic cannot leave you
When it is you.

What Is a Holiday Junkie?

Well, I explained how I became *the* Holiday Junkie, but I want to try and explain how anyone can tap into the Holiday Junkie energy. For me, celebrating, decorating, and creating moments of joy feels like something I *must* do. I know that the world will provide hard truths, scary realities, and teach us all lessons in its own unique ways. I know that my children will have broken hearts, hard conversations, and growing pains emotionally. So, for me, providing a little magic in our home feels like the least I can do. Within our walls is love, joy, magic, and imagination. Trust me, there's also stress, grumpy kids, mom guilt, and sometimes a good cry in the shower. But when I can pull off a feeling of wonder and belief in something special, that's when I feel like I've done right by my kids. Maybe it's because I had to grow up really fast, and held on to some extra little-kid vibes, but the magic feels so good. So, when you need to remember the whimsical, the magical, the glimmer in your heart that feels like the butterflies a kid gets on Christmas Eve, please remember you *can* find it. It's inside you, and waiting for you to reach back and grab it. I became the Holiday Junkie out of grief, and I stayed the Holiday Junkie out of belief. I just truly believe that the journey of life is easier with a little magic sprinkled in.

THE YEAR AS SEEN
BY THE HOLIDAY JUNKIE

JANUARY

The first two weeks of January are filled with the cleanup and put-away of memories made in the previous holiday season, and manifesting new energy for the new year. My best friend, Jenny, usually checks on me in that first week. The Holiday Junkie gets a little sad after all the festivities of the holidays come to an end. She knows me well.

On the first day of the new year, a family tradition since I was a kid, we make catfish, collard greens, and black-eyed peas to bring in abundance for the coming year! We open all the doors and sweep out the old energy and set intentions for new energy to find us. The kids love it because it feels magical and sets a tone of hope and excitement for the year to come.

By mid-January I am usually already into Valentine's mode, shopping for anything new to add to our décor and gathering things for the kids' Valentines boxes (I'll come back to that). February approaches our house with lots of excitement, and, of course, love!

FEBRUARY

I was actually supposed to be born on Valentine's Day! I came one week later, but was born with heart-shaped lips and named Love. For maybe too long in my childhood, I was convinced that Valentine's Day, or as I called it, Love Day, was made up for me. My mom didn't fight it. She would say, "Yep, it's Love Day!" It was hard to deny the holiday was meant for me with my name everywhere.

Decorations for Valentine's Day go up February 1. I give the kids love-themed boxes to enjoy, filled with heart-shaped glasses, love pajamas, kits to make classroom Valentines, some little sweet treat, and a soft stuffy friend who of course brings the love! Lego even has cute heart-themed builds. We also usually get crafty in February, and find cute crafts to make and send to Nana. It gives us bonding time, without the iPad, and Nana feels special. It's also her birthday month. On the big day, the 14th, we start the morning with little cards and tokens of love for the kids, and Brian and I exchange cards. He also gets me the most beautiful bouquet of flowers. Love Day is the best. Then one week later it's *my* big day, February 21! I love birthdays! It's a day of gratitude to my mom for laboring and raising me, and gratitude for being able to have this beautiful life, and for feeling excited about all the new things I will learn about myself in the coming year. Then the 26th is Margo's birthday. I have a wonderful mother-in-law and she deserves to feel extra special on her day, so we do what we can to make her feel the love!

The last day of February is strategy day! March is happening, and we have to catch a leprechaun!

MARCH

Come March 1, we are on Amazon and Etsy looking for trap supplies. We've been trying to catch this leprechaun for about five years now. They are *very* tricky, but we love making the traps. It's another great family project. We decorate with Popsicle sticks painted with rainbow colors; we leave Skittles, fake gold coins, pennies, boxes for traps, and we even made an awesome Magnatile tower once. On the morning of St Patrick's Day we wake up to a leprechaun disaster: toilet paper dragged through the hallway, green pee in the toilets, furniture pushed over, and the traps we made that he or she destroyed. So rude! We discuss our disappointment over Lucky Charms, and always decide that we will still try again next year. Like I said, they are tricky.

St Patty's Day is usually an adult holiday, but for us it's magical. We embrace the luck and have a family celebration with shamrock shakes. You can find great recipes on Pinterest. I strongly suggest making the day a magical family day, and seeing how lucky your kids feel that you celebrated with them.

The rest of March I go into pastel daydreams. Around March 21 the spring décor is in full effect, and I'm ready to hop into Easter weekend. (Sorry, holiday puns are my fave.)

APRIL

Flowers, bunnies, chocolate-covered eggs, and egg coloring are staples in our house. We always make egg decorating an after-school or weekend project, and the kids really love it. We also have an EggMazing machine! I highly suggest purchasing one ASAP! It spins the egg while you use markers to decorate. No mess and awesome-looking eggs. Easter décor really lends itself to over-the-top magic and whimsy. I will go deeper into this later and show you some pictures! We also love making Easter chow. It's a mix of all the yummy treats: powdered sugar, Chex cereal, and pretzels. It's a great gift for teachers, a snack surprise for school lunches, and a fun cooking project for you and your kids, or your kids and their friends.

After Easter has passed, I try to keep the magic going by planting seeds and watching them grow, as a fun way to celebrate Earth Day. The kids enjoy spring break friend time, aka bounce houses, ice cream, and sleeping in.

I truly believe this is where my Holiday Junkie spirit was born. Who is this excited about Easter at only one-year-old?! My mom loved this photo.

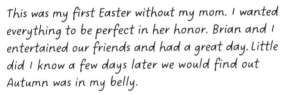

This was my first Easter without my mom. I wanted everything to be perfect in her honor. Brian and I entertained our friends and had a great day. Little did I know a few days later we would find out Autumn was in my belly.

MAY

Next, *May* I have your attention . . . Don't get me wrong, I love all the days in the year, because we are lucky to be alive and life is blessed. But other than a fun Cinco de Mayo dinner we do every year, this holiday lover uses May showers to clean and organize to pass time until the next celebration!

JUNE

This month starts with graduation decoration buying, the gathering of summer box items (I'll explain), and of course summer decorating! This means vintage surf décor, bright colors, and getting ready for summer camp! I always do a small celebration with caps and gowns for the kids when they get home from the last day of school, and they get those summer boxes I've been making.

Okay, so summer boxes are something I do for my kids every year. Items include water balloons, sunscreen, small pool toys, Polaroid cameras and film for summer memories, and vintage summer camp tees (found on Etsy). You get the idea. Be creative! At this point, I usually have a cabinet already filled with party decorations needed for Atticus and his big day! June 24 is his birthday, and he loves a party! So, while they start camp, I'm busy making gift bags with party favors, creating silly stations of fun little grab-and-go toys for the kids to enjoy, and getting my game plan down. I find that the more I can take off my plate, the more I can be a present and happy mommy on party day. As soon as the party is done, this Holiday Junkie takes the party down and puts up Fourth of July décor! I know, I'm crazy!

JULY

July starts with a bang! (I told you that holiday puns are my favorite.) I do love simple and pretty decorations for a fun weekend. We all love gathering in Mommy and Daddy's room, having a big sleepover, and watching the fireworks. The rest of July is, again, cleaning and gathering all my holiday energy, because from August until January I am in my happy place. A new holiday and celebration in every month until the end of the year means this holiday-addicted mommy doesn't stop!

AUGUST

It's a bit confusing for this fall lover, because even though it's not actually fall yet, pumpkins hit the stores and HomeGoods is filled with all the amber, brown, and gold décor you could dream of. So was born *early fall* in my house! I do a light sprinkling of fall-arriving décor and start making pumpkin cookies to fill the house with an amazing smell. Every day, I add a little more fall until our house has that magical feeling only fall provides! I am deeply connected to fall in my heart.

Of course, the most exciting part of August is Aidan's birthday! The 26th is a very special day for us to let our little magical guy know how happy we are that he joined our family. He loves to say "Happy Birthday," loves a party, and his siblings really love celebrating him, so it's super fun for all of us.

Even though fall doesn't actually begin until the middle of September, I follow the yearly holiday calendar of Starbucks. As the clock strikes midnight on August 31, Starbucks and I believe Pumpkin Spice season begins! For me, that signals that it's officially fall!

SEPTEMBER

Okay, this month is full-blown pumpkin patches, Pumpkin Spice, and my favorite maple light up trees are on all day until bedtime. And because I have a holiday decorating calendar to follow, I am of course already gathering, planning, envisioning, and prepping for October 1 when Halloween goes up! We spend

FARMERS Market
EST LOCAL

weekends and afternoons doing crafts to send to Nana, and I start gathering our pumpkins for Washi pumpkins (which I will tell you more about in October). Autumn loves fall because it's also known as autumn, and she loves hearing her name everywhere, much like her mama and Valentine's Day (Love Day). On the last day of October, fall décor is put away until what I call *second fall* (I'll explain that in November), and the kids wait with anticipation until our house becomes a Halloween explosion!

OCTOBER

Boo! One of the coolest things about my husband is that he was born on Halloween! So, naturally, we go crazy in October. Tons of festivities, crafting, baking treats, and silly scary energy goes all month long to celebrate our special guy! One tradition that my kids love is when I make everyone a special pumpkin; hand-painted and decorated like a character they choose. It's so much fun and they absolutely love it. You can buy cool kits at Target and on Amazon that make it super easy.

We also do Washi pumpkins. When Autumn and Atticus were very small, I didn't want them carving pumpkins or using glue and paint, which would make a mess, so I taught them how to do Washi pumpkins. Just buy Washi tape and apply the strips to your pumpkins to make your own design. They're super long lasting; we repurpose ours in November. (I'll come back to that.)

On Halloween we always have a party for the kids with trick-or-treat stations, yummy food, over-the-top decorations, and a pumpkin pie for Brian (he doesn't like cake). After a birthday wish and a toast, we all go out for trick-or-treating and Halloween joy. It's lights out at 8:30 pm and sweet witchy dreams for all!

NOVEMBER

Oh, how I love you, November! This is where that *second fall* that we talked about comes in. It's time for the fall decorations I didn't put out in August. It has more of a Thanksgiving, "be thankful" feel, and is very warm and cozy vibes. It's also the time when I redo all the pumpkins and make them new again. The Washi tape we used for Halloween peels off easily. I take off the tape, paint the orange pumpkins in yummy fall colors, and then usually use some gold foil or glitter (found at Michaels) to give them a warm fall sparkle. You can wrap lights around them, or don't. They're an amazing addition to put on a bar or cabinet for warmth and celebration.

Oh, and we can't forget the elves! Candy Cane (Atticus's elf), Tinsel (Autumn's elf), and Fig (Aidan's elf) arrive on the 24th because they hate missing Autumn's birthday. Following the elves' antics all the way to Christmas can be exhausting, but I love it, and so do they.

Then it's time for Autumn's big day! November 26, we celebrate our girl. Her party is usually thrown a couple of weeks before or after her actual birthday because it falls so close to Turkey Day. She loves her birthday, and as she gets older, she's already showing big signs of a future Holiday Junkie. She's awesome to brainstorm with for her party dreams and is very helpful with putting it all together. I do enjoy a quiet moment after her birthday to take everything down, deep clean, and take a breath before it's time for Big Claus Energy!

DECEMBER

Okay, let's dive into the most magical month of all, but also the most emotionally complicated. This month requires the most energy, tradition, grace, understanding, fun, love, and belief in magic. It's pure, it's enchanting, it's exciting, and it brings as much joy as sadness, because for every one person who is feeling connection, another is feeling loss. For every couple in love, someone is also lonely. For every perfect family, there is a broken one. Yet the music, traditions, lights, and festivities somehow, in one moment or another, help us hope, have faith, or believe, and that is beautiful. That is the essence of *magic*.

Our December is full of all the joy and magic I can find and make happen in our home. Our house has not one room that didn't get the Go Big or Go Home Christmas Memo. I truly believe Ancestry.com holds the proof of me being a descendant of either an elf or Claus himself. It's my favorite time of year, and yet still holds for me at least three mom breakdowns of "Can I get it all wrapped and done in time?" and one big I-miss-my-mom cry in the shower, but it always works out.

The chaos turns into gatherings of laughter and good wishes, snuggles, cookies, and holiday movies, and although it's sad to say goodbye to the elves, it means the big guy is on his way. As my babies search the skies on Christmas Eve for a sign of reindeer and Santa, I search for a sign that my mom is with us. That night's sleep, if you can call it that, has an energy that's unlike any other night of the year. Christmas Day is finally here and, well, that's the kids' day to finally enjoy all their wishes and

hopes that come true and for us to just provide batteries and loving support and . . . coffee. Lots of coffee. That night we have a family dinner and then pass out with a magic hangover. It's perfect. It's *magic*.

Jenny usually checks on me again around the 28th, because she knows that with only one holiday left this year, the Holiday Junkie is feeling down or exhausted or both. I, of course, bring out the sparkle, disco balls, sparkling apple cider, and champagne for New Year's Eve! It's a family affair with any other families who want to go to bed at 10 pm. We dance, manifest, reflect, eat, and do the early Netflix New Year's Eve Countdown for kids!

That's how the Holiday Junkie does a year. Time flies when you're having fun!

Three generations of Holiday Junkies. My G-ma had so much holiday spirit and loved making the holidays special. My mom inherited her mom's holiday magic-making and then passed it to me. We all made magic differently for our families but the special love we all shared for being festive remained the same.

How to Embrace a Holiday Junkie

1. Being driven by holiday spirit and magic-making is real. Don't judge.
2. Glitter is a nightmare, but we must have glitter, and vacuum later.
3. Don't be afraid to admit when even *you* get caught up in the magic. Just let go and enjoy.
4. Never point out that decorating is stressful or makes us grumpy. We like to believe it's 24/7 glimmer and that we are delightful.
5. Always give a hug, kiss, or sweet note to acknowledge all that went into creating the magic.
6. Yes, we can make anything a celebration or holiday, so just embrace it.
7. The trees, lights, extra-large Santa, giant spiders, and extra storage unit for these things are actually needed.
8. Your kids will never forget what holidays and birthdays looked like growing up, and they will pass the magic along to your grandchildren. Promise. So let it all happen.
9. The world will provide all the hard truths, scary lessons, and heartbreak that's needed for all of us to grow. Make your home safe, magical, and happy.
10. Never go to a HomeGoods, Target, Michaels, or Hobby Lobby without asking us to go with you, especially when holiday décor is on the shelves.
11. Never ask us if we need "all that wrapping paper?!" Of course we do!

And lastly:

Everyone needs a Holiday Junkie in their life. So let us just be our silly, magical, over-the-top, deep-believing, sometimes stressed and grumpy holiday selves, and just enjoy!

Oh My Gourd!

All right, I promised a Washi explanation, and a breakdown of how I use pumpkins from September until after Thanksgiving! The Washi started because I'm a neat freak, and couldn't wrap my head around the messy pumpkin carving of it all with small kids involved. So I decided to try seeing if Washi tape would stick to a pumpkin. It did and looked fabulous! Kids love using Washi tape because it's so easy, and it's now one of our favorite activities every year.

Grab some tape, make a pattern, or just let your creative juices flow, and you have an awesome pumpkin with very little mess.

Another fun and magical way to do this is to make it a party! With a small table set up, put various colored and patterned Washi tape in bowls in the center. Two or three small pumpkins for each kid should be good. I also put out a snack board or snack bowls in the middle of the table, because being creative can make you hungry. After the pumpkins are done, let the kids make a Halloween bark to eat together or take home. Halloween bark is melting chocolate, pretzels, candies, and sprinkles together. Let it harden and eat! (You can find recipes anywhere if you don't want to improvise.) Just like that, you've created magic and made memories!

The pumpkin makeover is one of the best times of year for me. It's creative and relaxing because I love to paint and create, and it's so fun to keep the pumpkin love going right through Turkey Day. Sometimes I'll do dark greens, navy, and various blue tones or even go chocolate brown and deep reds with gold foil and glitter. I love to add light-up branches or strings of lights to really make them pop, and it's usually a credenza centerpiece for us. So, here's how I do it.

First of all, the Washi tape peels off! Thank you, Washi! I take off the tape from our Halloween mini ones and now have new pumpkins to decorate. Because I haven't carved and messed with the big pumpkins I have, I can add paint and make them all new again. I wipe them down and get ready to paint. I love painting the ones with texture and knots because it looks so cool. It takes two to three coats of craft paint, depending on how dark the orange is on your pumpkins. If that seems too time-consuming, choose a darker color as your palette. Also, white pumpkins are great, but if you go pastel with your colors it can take a few coats. The gold foil, paints, and glitter spray or flakes, I get at Michaels, and you can probably find them at any craft store. The gold foil is so fun. You can watch tutorials online for how to use it, but I promise it's so easy. Messy but beautiful. (Gold foil not recommended for kids, though!)

Here's one more idea for my pumpkin lovers, high on fun and also high on mess. It's paint-pour pumpkins. This is a great activity for an adult pumpkin party, with snacks, appetizers, and good cheer, or something to try as your kids get older. Buy a bunch of paint, some plastic to cover the table or the ground, and some

plastic cups to put paint in, and go for it! Put as many colors as you want in one cup and then pour it over the pumpkins. Let the paint dry for a bit and pour again if you want. There are a plethora of tutorials online for inspiration, but there's really no wrong way to do it. It makes for a groovy pumpkin and will for sure stand out! I know all of your creations will be GOURDgeous!

Let's Make a Holiday Plan

The key element for any holiday or party is *the plan.* Prep is key to not only making the event or holiday amazing, but also leaving some space for you to enjoy the process. I'm searching Pinterest, Instagram, and Etsy pretty much daily, and when I find a theme, color, vibe, or idea I love, it's saved ASAP. I create folders

Left: This is a stolen moment for a sleepy but happy mommy on Christmas morning. (Not pictured: the sound of new toys and Christmas music.) *Right:* This is what I call a Christmas miracle. A good picture of this Party of Five looking cute and festive together. (Not pictured: the complaining and craziness of trying to get one pic.)

with lots of ideas that I can pull from when I need to: anything from décor to dessert ideas, themes, food boards, party favors, and so on.

Then I look at things I have coming up. Usually I will start planning and gathering everything I need at least two months before the date of the event. I know that sounds crazy and, yes, my family agrees. But it allows me to stress so much less on the actual day, and enjoy the moment. I do leave room for last-minute magical finds, but I know where I'm headed and what I'm creating. Christmas gets easier every year, because we keep adding little things to what is now our yearly décor. But I do try to change up little things from year to year, like the placement of the décor, or by adding a theme just to make it feel new in small ways.

As an example, here's the way I break down a holiday party:

1. Theme
2. Décor ideas
3. Holiday activities for adults and kids
4. Go caroling or hire carolers
5. Magical touches for holiday spirit (sweets, holiday crafts, or go big with fake snow)

Holiday prep is all about reminding yourself of everything you already have to work with. I forget I have things every year, and then buy new stuff when I don't have to, which is why I now have forty glitter houses (but the truth is I love them so it's a win). Go back to the folders you've been filling with your online searches to choose themes, vibes, and colors. Last year I did a pastel Christmas theme in one room and a vintage Christmas vibe in the main room. Autumn wanted a modern girly vibe, and the boys wanted an old-school feel. Everyone was happy and it was so fun, but it couldn't have happened if I waited till the last minute to do everything. I always save room in a Christmas theme for our special touches: Autumn's art, Atticus's holiday Legos, and anything Brian and I have collected in our years together. Aidan will be adding his own touches soon, but for now, at age twenty-one months, he goes with the flow.

Again, if you start planning in your mind early, then when it's time to decorate you can stay in a happy place. My husband will tell you that I can get moody around decorating time. It's so fun, but also stressful trying to make your vision come to life. I've gotten better at doing the prep work, so I don't have too many apologies to make after the magic has landed in the right places.

This is what helps me. Make decorating and planning your own; find the balance between stressed, joyful, overwhelmed, and present. I know that can be tough. I hope some of these ideas help. Now go make magic!

Big Claus Energy

I take my holiday energy very seriously. Even when I have been sick or grieving, the magic of December truly brings me back to life. By the way, as I write this, we have 201 days, 14 hours, 37 minutes, and 14 seconds till Christmas. Yes, I track it all year! Don't judge me. I have often said that perhaps somewhere in my DNA I could be part elf. I still check the skies every December 24 just in case the little girl in me was correct. And, of course, as a mom, I dive deep into magic, tradition, decorations, and everything that brings Big Claus Energy to life. I love that for a moment in time we all believe in the same idea. Maybe not all in the same way, and some more than others, but we all in one way or another feel the spirit of the end-of-year holidays. We try harder with kindness and selflessness. We sing the songs, bake the cookies, get the trees, watch the movies, and we feel a deeper need to let magic in.

Even for non-believers or for people who the holidays bring pain, the perfect Christmas moment is still possible because it's a magical time of year. I have always loved Christmas. As a child, I remember my mom glowing differently during that time of year. I felt more kindness and connection with people. I longed for the deep belief that as I slept magical things were happening not just for me but everyone.

You don't have to be part of a particular culture or religion to experience that feeling. Toasting with my husband's famous Christmas cocktail after the tree is done, him sitting in his chair and reading surrounded by the warm glow of lights, and us sleeping among our decorations, fills my heart with joy and gives me such a comforting feeling in our traditions. As I get older, I'm always searching for ways to create that same feeling at other times throughout the year. I use decorating as a chance to show my gratitude for being able to celebrate and create magic, whatever the season. When Brian texts me saying how beautiful it all looks, and when I see my kids take in all the hope, magic, and real joy that's around them, it makes me feel so proud. I know that, somehow, we've captured what the spirit is. What an incredible gift that we get to do this every year!

The Twelve ~~Days~~ *Ideas* of Christmas *Decorating* (Holiday Junkie Style)

1. Decorate and create the vibe. This is *my* job! I love to take input from everyone in the family, and then get them working on something else. This Holiday Junkie needs space to decorate.
2. Christmas family movie time. The kids are in charge of making movie tickets and setting up everyone's seats.
3. Invite friends over for a kid- and adult-friendly holiday crafting hang. Cocktails for the grown-ups.
4. Host a holiday party to see everyone before they travel. We always have carolers! Or go caroling if that's your thing!
5. Take a holiday drive through the neighborhood to see the lights. Bring hot chocolate and cookies for extra cheer. (Everyone wears festive pajamas, of course!)
6. Tree time! In our house Daddy does the lights. Kids and Mommy join in for ornaments. Brian and I always toast to our tree with his famous holiday cocktail. (See chapter three, "Recipe Magic," for details . . . and enjoy!)
7. Set up a writing table for letters to Santa and card-making. Encourage creativity and, of course, make sure you mail everything.
8. Christmas cookie time! Some for us and some for Santa!
9. Decorate mini trees for the kids' rooms. They get to be in charge.

10. We like to have a Christmas sleepover in our bedroom. Lots of Christmas books to read, and lots of snuggling.

11. Set aside some private wrap time for Mama while everyone sleeps! Like a real elf. The presents are wrapped, and the joy is ready to be shared. It's my favorite time to put on *The Holiday* or *Love Actually* and remind myself of what we *actually* ordered everyone!

12. Christmas Eve and Christmas Day are always magical. For me, they also have sad moments because I miss my mom so much. We have tamales on Christmas Eve, a tradition that started as a kid for me. On Christmas Day, Brian makes pasta or sometimes we will do a roast.

I try to make December a true celebration of magic, love, tradition, and enjoying the final days of the year! May some of our ideas inspire your new memories.

Countdown to Magic

Okay, New Year's Eve has changed a lot for us since having kids. But in the last few years I feel like we have found a great way to party *family style*. The key for us was finding other families that were game to create a new way to have fun! New Year's Eve, for us, looks like this:

I decorate, of course, that morning: disco balls. Gold, black, and shiny. We make a photo wall in our big window for New Year's pics! We also make vision boards over breakfast by clipping out pics from magazines, printing pics from the internet, and using kits that come with great words and stickers. It's a great way to be creative and spend time with your kids, but also see what they envision for the new year and how they are feeling about the year they are leaving behind.

Shopping first, then . . .

We do special grocery shopping for January 1. Since I was a kid, on the 1st we've always eaten catfish, black-eyed peas, and collard greens for good luck in the new year. My kids don't love it, to be honest, but Brian and I do.

It's time to get ready and party! I usually do a chili bar on New Year's Eve because it's an easy and delicious dinner, and even the kids like it.

Our New Year's Eve party starts at 4 pm. I know, we really know how to party! We have welcome cocktails for adults and Martinelli's sparkling cider for the kids to toast. The chili bar is ready, and the kitchen counter is filled with snacks for kids: a charcuterie board, dips, chips, and all the fixings for chili. The kids usually do some sort of dance party, and every family gets a chance for a great end-of-the-year photo on our photo wall. It's a big hangout time and really makes my heart full to end the year with people we love, eating, drinking, laughing, and dancing together.

Then, between 8 pm and 9 pm, we do an early countdown for the kids. And, who am I kidding, also for me! Everyone gets to hug and kiss for our early midnight, and it's lights out for the Hallisay household by 9:30 or 10 pm. New Year's Eve brings a weird feeling of not knowing what the new year will bring, and sometimes feeling like you didn't get all you wanted out of the year that's leaving us. But the magic is in the gratitude for the year you've been given, and the hope for the year ahead.

That's just how we do it for now. I know that one day our kids will want to be somewhere else with their friends, or Brian and I will go out somewhere and come home in time to kiss our babies before midnight. But for now, in this special pocket of time, celebrating the new year means us being together with great friends, and it's magic!

MAGIC-MAKERS AND HOLIDAY JUNKIE ICONS

C heck out these amazing companies, and I hope all your parties and holidays are magical.

2021 Co.
@2021_co
2021co.com

Bon Puf
@bonpuf
bonpuf.com

Bonjour Fête
@bonjourfete
bonjourfete.com

Christopher Radko
@christopher.radko
christopherradko.com

Cody Bonham
@block_and_knife
blockandknife.etsy.com

Create Room
@createroomco
createroom.com

Dip'd n Drip'd
@dipd_n_dripd
dipdndripd.com

Elisabeth + Faith
@elisabethandfaith
elisabethandfaith.com

Ellie and Piper
@ellieandpiperco
ellieandpiper.com

Fleurs Et Sel
@fleursetsel
fleursetsel.com

Get Caked LA
@getcakedla
getcakedla.com

Glitterville Studios
@glittervilleholidaypop
glitterville.com

Good Carma Studio
@goodcarmastudio
goodcarmastudio.com

Gourmeletas
@gourmeletas
gourmeletas.com

Haute Hop
@haute_hop

Hobby Lobby
@hobbylobby
hobbylobby.com

Holiday Warehouse
@holidaywarehouse
holidaywarehouse.com

Home Goods
@homegoods
homegoods.com

Judith March
@judithmarch
judithmarch.com

Little Artist Party
@little_artist_party
littleartistparty.com

Little Horse on the Prairie
@littlehorseontheprairie
littlehorseontheprairie.net

Meri Meri
@merimeriparty
merimeri.com

MESH kids co.
@meshkidsco
meshkids.co

Michaels
@michaelsstores
michaels.com

Minnidip
@minnidip
minnidip.com

Paper Source
@papersouce
papersource.com

Peace of Mind Designs
@peaceofminddesignssc
peaceofmind-designs.com

Platinum Prop House
@platinumprophouse
platinumprophouse.com

Sami Riccioli
@sami_riccioli
samiriccioli.com

Shavs Paper
@shavspaper
shavspaper.com

Stoney Clover Lane
@stoneyclover
stoneycloverlane.com

Target
@target
target.com

Teak and Lace
@teakandlace
teakandlace.com

The Balloon Cart
@theballooncartco
theballooncartco.com

The Picnic Collective
@thepicnic.collective
thepicniccollective.com

ThePinkHutch
@thepinkhutch
thepinkhutch.com

Vanessa Rivera
@the_life_of_aivax
linktr.ee/the_life_of_aivax

Wings and Stardust
@wingsandstardust
ko-fi.com/wingsandstardust

WonderTent Parties
@wondertentparties
wondertentparties.com

YearCheer
@yearcheer
yearcheer.com

Young + Wild and Friedman
@youngwildandfriedman
youngwildandfriedman.com

THANK YOU

I am so deeply grateful I got to write this book. It allowed me deeper healing from my grief, to feel closer to my mom, and to introduce her to all of you. I feel so excited that maybe one person will be inspired to add a little magic in a new way to their life. I hold the deepest gratitude to all the magic-makers in my life. You know who you are. Thank you for inspiring me every day and, when the world pushes us not to believe, for making more magic. I am so grateful for little moments of curious wonder, proof that magic can be created and deeply felt, and for Autumn, Atticus, and Aidan, who remind me daily that seeing things in a magical way is the best way.

Thank you to Nina, Adam, Monica, and BenBella for supporting me and helping this dream come true. Vanessa, your talent and art elevated this book in such a special way. Nicole, you are my editing angel and have truly been my eyes on this entire book. I couldn't have done it without you. To my husband, Brian, for believing in me and making magic possible every day. To my best friend, Jenny. You had so many good times with my mom and her magic, and she loved you so deeply. Your friendship has been one of the greatest gifts in my life. I love you. To Gans, who saw how happy holidays made me and for telling me a long time ago to do something with it. To Laura, for always letting me read you things as they were written and embracing the magic. To my friends who always show up and celebrate with us. You know it's my happy place and you support this Holiday Junkie with so much love. To my nieces, Campbell, Eleanora, Juliet, and Hallie; and my nephew, Coleman. I hope magic finds you every day. To Margo, Meghan, and Michelle. Thank you for the recipes and support for this book. I love you. To my brother, Todd, thanks for just being you. Life as your sister has been magical. To all of you reading this, thank you for letting me fill these pages with my heart, my stories, ideas, and deep belief in all things sparkly, fun, whimsical, and of course magical.

I hope this book inspires you to become your own magic-maker and Holiday Junkie.

All my love,
JLH

MY MAGIC

As I said at the beginning of this book—magic found me in my childhood, but saved me through my grief, reminding me of how things could be special again, blessed, and of course *magical.*

I'm able to be with my mom in a new way by creating magic that she has left for me.

I remember being twelve years old, and my only wish was to be a mom. I knew nothing about motherhood except that I wanted to give a child the same magical, warm fuzzy feeling my mom gave me. I was very young to know that at the time, but I always think that that's how special my mom was. At a young age I already knew that what she was giving me, and what we shared, was the most profound love and magic possible. I strive to create that with my children every day, and in creating magic for them I, too, am passing it on.

If I'm being honest, I don't know if my mom's magic has fully become my own. I feel like I still borrow from her magic daily, but I do know that my husband, my kids, and myself get through this life a little bit easier with the help of my inherited magic.

ABOUT THE AUTHOR

Jennifer Love Hewitt is an actress, singer, director, producer, and author. She is known for her film and television acting, including roles in the *I Know What You Did Last Summer* franchise, *Party of 5*, *Ghost Whisperer*, and *The Client List*. She currently stars in the procedural drama *9-1-1* on ABC. Her book on relationships, *The Day I Shot Cupid*, was published by Hyperion in 2010, becoming a *New York Times* bestseller the week of its release.

A lot has changed in Jennifer's life, including the passing of her mother, getting married, becoming the mother of three kids, and launching her brand, The Holiday Junkie.